The

Illusion

of

Light

The

Illusion

of

Light

Thinking after the Enlightenment

Bry Willis

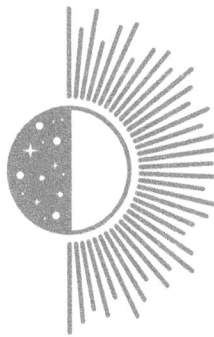

PHILOSOPHICS PRESS ◐ 2025

FIRST EDITION

Originally developed as the introductory work to *The Anti-Enlightenment Essays* series:

Objectivity Is Illusion (2025)

Rational Ghosts (2025)

Temporal Ghosts (2025)

Against Agency (2025)

The Myth of *Homo Normalis* (2025)

The Discipline of Dis-Integration (2025)

The *Anti-Enlightenment Essays* series explores the limits and afterlives of Enlightenment rationality in modern thought.

Published by *PHILOSOPHICS PRESS*, Cambridge, Massachusetts

Printed in the country of distribution

philosophics.blog

ISBN 978-0-9710869-3-7 (cloth)

ISBN 978-0-9710869-7-5 (paperback)

LCCN: Pending

Subject Keywords:

Enlightenment – Philosophy.

Knowledge, Theory of.

Reason – History.

Civilisation, Modern – Philosophy.

Ethics – Philosophy.

Philosophy, Modern – Criticism and interpretation.

"The Enlightenment was never a dawn; it was a flash – brilliant, disorienting, and still leaving afterimages."

— Bry Willis, The Discipline of Dis-Integration

"Dare to know! Have the courage to use your own understanding."

— Immanuel Kant, 'What Is Enlightenment?' (1784)

DEDICATION

For those still learning to see in the dark.

ACKNOWLEDGEMENTS

With thanks to those who taught me that maintenance is a form of thought, and that care is its own philosophy.

To Nietzsche, who broke the sun;
to Proudhon, who refused the master's logic;
to Sartre and Kafka, who mapped the interior shadows;
to Zapffe and Benatar, who faced the void with composure.
Their questions remain the scaffolding beneath these pages.

Contents

The Myth of Illumination

The House of Reason

Living after the Light

Appendices

Preface – Reading by Residual Light

To read these essays is to move slowly from the glare into the dimmer spaces where things regain texture. The Enlightenment taught us to equate light with truth, but illumination has always been double-edged: it clarifies outlines whilst erasing depth. What disappears in the brightness are the gradients – the in-between shades where thought and feeling meet, where contradiction still breathes.

The half-light is not a retreat from knowledge; it is where knowledge stops mistaking itself for salvation. It is the hour before dawn and after dusk, when perception is most alert, and everything seems both clearer and less certain. That is the discipline these essays practice: a sustained attentiveness to what persists when certainty burns away.

This project does not ask readers to abandon reason, only to notice what it has excluded. It invites a kind of intellectual night vision – the patience to see without spotlight, the willingness to sit with what does not resolve. In the half-light, the world no longer arranges itself around the human gaze; it reveals itself as unmastered, partial, alive.

Here, we will learn to dwell in that half-light – not as a retreat from knowledge, but as a discipline of seeing what the Enlightenment's glare erased.

The Enlightenment promised that truth would make us free. Perhaps it made us efficient instead. What these pages attempt is smaller and slower: a freedom measured not in control but in composure – the ability to live with what cannot be fixed, to keep tending meaning after its foundations have collapsed.

If there is light here, it is not the triumphant blaze of discovery but the ambient glow that remains after something ends. It's the light of screens left on overnight, of cities at rest, of the mind still thinking long after certainty has gone to sleep.

Step carefully. Let your eyes adjust. The world looks different when it stops pretending to be illuminated.

PART I

THE
MYTH OF ILLUMINATION

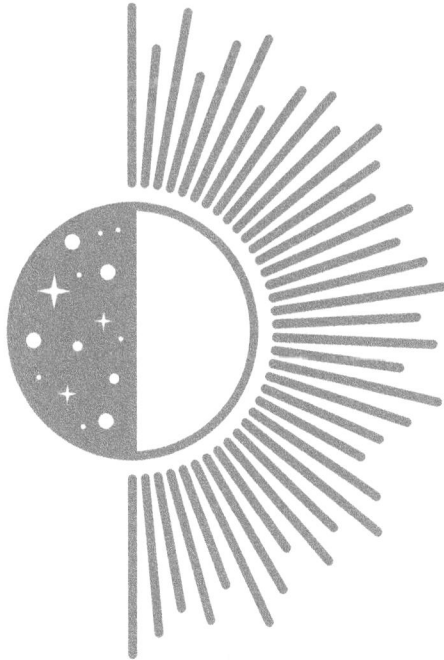

ONE

Before the Switch Was Flipped

The Enlightenment named itself. That alone should make us suspicious. To call oneself 'enlightened' is to claim not just knowledge, but moral authority – the power to define what counts as light, and what must be left in the dark.

Movements rarely survive their own branding, and this one began with a marketing campaign: the Age of Light, the Century of Reason. Like the 'Holy Roman Empire', it was neither singular, holy, nor especially reasonable. But the label stuck, and with it came a myth so pervasive that even its detractors speak its language.

The trick was simple. To call oneself enlightened, one first had to invent the dark. The centuries that preceded it – rich with theology, cosmology, and craft – were recast as the Middle Ages, a tunnel between ignorance and understanding, superstition and science. The metaphor of light made this hierarchy feel natural. To step from shadow into illumination became not only progress but salvation. And like all conversions, it demanded testimony: the recitation of what we had been delivered from.

Yet the story was never that clean. The so-called Dark Ages produced universities, cathedrals, astronomical theories, scholastic logics, and the first stirrings of humanism. What the Enlightenment offered was not revelation but rebranding: the same hunger for order and transcendence, dressed now in the vocabulary of clarity. Reason replaced faith; progress replaced grace. The creed remained – only its scripture changed.

Even this 'Enlightenment' was less a dawn than a patchwork of small, conflicting fires.

In Scotland, the light was empirical, patient, civic – Hume doubting everything, Smith measuring sympathy.

In France, it was theatrical and moral – a revolution staged in prose, the dream of a universal reason marching toward virtue.

In Germany, it was metaphysical, stern, self-examining – Kant's light so blinding it cast a bureaucracy of the mind.

In England, it was mercantile and cautious – the glow of a counting-house lamp, bright enough to guide ships and laws, dim enough to leave empire in the shadows.

Each claimed to be the true flame. Each burned differently.

Later historians folded this dissonance into a single beam, flattening the quarrel into harmony. Thus, was born The Enlightenment, capitalised and coherent, a story we still tell ourselves to feel awake. We speak of it as if the world once slept and then, suddenly, thought. But there was no switch, no dawn chorus – only the slow adjustment of eyes already straining to see.

I am not writing history. I am describing an afterimage: the lingering glare that still defines what we call modern.

The Enlightenment's light was dazzling, but like all glares, it left afterimages – outlines too sharp to touch, shadows too deep to name. It taught us to see the world as something to be mapped, measured, managed; to treat darkness not as mystery but as error. Its illumination was never gentle. It burned away nuance and shadow, left outlines too sharp to touch. And we, its descendants, are still blinking.

This project – these essays – begin from that squint. To write against the Enlightenment is not to curse its brightness but to study its residue: the way it flattened thought into geometry, morality into calculus, care into code. We have lived too long in its fluorescent hum. *The Illusion of Light* is not a call to switch it off, only to notice how much of the world's texture disappeared in its glare.

TWO

The Promised Light

The Enlightenment promised deliverance. Its gospel was reason; its miracle, progress. Humanity, it said, had come of age. No more priests between us and truth, no more kings between us and law, no more shadows between us and light. The world would finally make sense – if only we learned to think correctly.

But even in its first sermons, there were fissures. The apostles of this new illumination could not agree on what the light revealed. Some saw the geometry of nature, others the sovereignty of man, still others the invisible hand arranging both. Reason, depending on who invoked it, could justify rebellion or obedience, equality or hierarchy, atheism or providence. It was less a revelation than a mirror: each thinker saw in its glow what they most wished to be true.

In Paris, Diderot and Voltaire imagined reason as theatre – a spectacle of emancipation where superstition was laughed off the stage. Their *Encyclopédie* became scripture for the literate class, a promise that all knowledge could be catalogued, ordered, cross-referenced into coherence. Across the Channel, Locke's empiricism had already turned thought into property: what the mind perceived, it could possess. Kant, ever the system-builder, drew the lines that would confine both: the categories of understanding, the bounds of reason, the tidy architecture of the possible.

Each flame cast its own shadow. The moral geometry of Kant would soon solidify into bureaucracy and law. Smith's sympathetic economics would harden into market theology. The *Encyclopédie*'s dream of universal knowledge would find its perfection in the algorithm – an index without comprehension. Even Hume's gentle scepticism, meant to humble the mind, became the foundation for positivism, which humbled nothing at all.

Still, the rhetoric of illumination was irresistible. Light became our civilisation's universal metaphor for good – clarity, transparency, innovation, openness. The brighter the world became, the less we noticed what was bleaching out of view. Our language filled with its glow: enlightenment, insight, oversight, oversight committee. We named our devices after it, then our ethics, then ourselves.

Those who questioned the glare were dismissed as romantics or reactionaries. The age's critics – Blake, Kierkegaard, Nietzsche, Weber – were not enemies of reason but witnesses to its exhaustion. They saw that the light of progress had turned sterile, its rational heat consuming what it once claimed to warm. They were, in their way, the first anti-enlightened: not advocates of darkness, but defenders of shadow – the place where complexity, contradiction, and meaning survive.

That is where these essays live. Not in the dark, and not in the glare, but somewhere in the uncertain penumbra between. They begin from the recognition that the Enlightenment's promise was never false, only overexposed. The light did reveal; it also erased. To write against it is not to deny its brilliance, but to recall what it blinded us to: that the human mind needs shade as much as sight.

The Enlightenment sought to abolish night. The Anti-Enlightenment learns again to see by starlight.

THREE

The Economy of Illumination

Every civilisation invents a story to explain its hunger. Ours chose light. We learned to call knowledge illumination, and soon after, to treat illumination as capital. What began as a metaphor of awakening became a market in revelation. The Enlightenment did not simply praise reason; it privatised it. What began as a metaphor of awakening became a market in revelation – one that still shapes how we value thought, attention, and even ourselves. Thought, once a commons of inquiry, was divided, fenced, and titled in the name of expertise. From patents to publishing houses, the glow was parcelled into tradable property – every bright idea a claim of ownership on the invisible.

The logic persists. The modern economy is no longer powered by coal or steam but by cognition itself – by the extraction and exchange of attention, creativity, and the shimmer of insight. We still burn to keep the lights on, only now the fuel is human consciousness. What Proudhon once called cognitive rent – the fee extracted for access to the means of thinking – has become the organising principle of the digital age. Universities, media, and markets all operate on the same moral arithmetic: enlightenment as subscription.

It is tempting to see this as corruption, a betrayal of pure reason by commerce. But that distinction is another illusion. The Enlightenment was already an economy. Every academy and encyclopaedia it produced was a factory of light – converting curiosity into authority, wonder into wage. The difference between knowledge and capital was never categorical, only rhetorical. 'Sapere aude,' dare to know, meant also dare to own, to publish, to profit.

To understand the present, we must follow that transaction to its conclusion. The light has become self-employing. Each of us is now a subcontractor in the economy of illumination, producing our own transparency – profiling, posting, curating the visible self. The glare has gone internal. Reason, once a social contract, is now a gig.

The market learned early that light attracts. The same curiosity that filled lecture halls also filled ledgers. What the Church once sold as indulgence, the modern state sold as education, and later the corporation as innovation. Each promised emancipation through access to illumination – each erected new tolls at the gates of knowing. Weber understood this when he wrote of the 'iron cage' of rationalisation: a world where the promise of mastery becomes its own enclosure. Foucault merely extended the insight – knowledge and power no longer oppose each other; they circulate, indistinguishable, as energy within the same grid. What we call progress is often just the efficiency of that current.

In the old economy, wealth was measured by accumulation; in the new, by illumination – by how much of the world one can render visible, calculable, administrable. Data replaces gold as the emblem of stored light. Yet the extraction remains the same: people mined not for minerals but for meaning. The Enlightenment's moral vocabulary – clarity, evidence, transparency – becomes the alibi for surveillance and speculation alike. Under the banner of reason, we have built a system that never sleeps, that insists everything must be lit, even the private corners where thought once gestated in the dark.

This is not conspiracy but continuity. Every epoch believes it has left superstition behind, unaware that its own faith has simply changed medium. The medieval tithed to God; the modern pays rent to knowledge. Subscription replaces salvation. The metrics are new, but the theology remains: revelation as reward, darkness as debt. What began as a metaphor of emancipation ends as a compulsion to perform enlightenment – always learning, always improving, always exposed. Even ignorance has become productive; it is the raw material for correction, the darkness that justifies more light.

Yet, as with all economies, there are limits to growth. The light begins to cannibalise itself. We flood the world with so much information that understanding becomes impossible; attention collapses under the weight of its own illumination. The glare becomes blindness again, but this time with receipts. To live in such a world is to pay perpetually for the privilege of seeing nothing clearly.

Eventually, every economy confronts the cost of its own abundance. The Enlightenment promised infinite growth in the currency of light, but even photons fatigue the eye. We have reached the saturation point where seeing more reveals less, where knowing more produces paralysis. The dream of total visibility – scientific, moral, informational – has inverted into its opposite: the opaque glow of overload. The light is no longer a medium of understanding but a solvent, bleaching depth into surface.

In this glare, the old hierarchies of ignorance and expertise collapse. Everyone knows enough to speak and too much to listen. Every utterance competes for wattage. Even dissent becomes monetised as a brand of enlightenment, outrage as another colour in the spectrum of reason's commerce. The marketplace of ideas, once imagined as public agora, has become a carnival of light, each booth brighter than the last, none illuminating more than its own stall.

And yet, exhaustion itself begins to suggest another ethic. Fatigue can clarify what fervour conceals. When illumination becomes unbearable, one begins to crave shadow again – not ignorance, but reprieve. The eye adjusts, learns to value dimness as precision. What emerges is not rejection of the Enlightenment but recovery from it: a slow adaptation to partial vision, to thought that need not be fully lit to be lucid.

That adaptation is the task of the afterimage – the moment when the light fades but its memory persists, pulsing behind closed eyes. It is there, in the phosphorescent residue of reason, that philosophy must now learn to dwell. For the glare has done its work; what remains is to live wisely among the remnants of its glow.

Every light needs a fixture. The Enlightenment built its own – a house of Reason designed to contain the radiance it had conjured. Its walls were logic, its windows transparency, its roof a promise of progress. Each century merely redecorated. The philosophers called it order, the economists equilibrium, the politicians consent. Even the critics, unable to live outdoors, took up residence in the ruins.

We have grown used to this architecture. Its angles define what we mean by sense itself; its corridors organise our speech. Yet the structure groans. The plaster of progress flakes. The floorboards of agency warp. The air smells faintly of ozone, as if some bulb has been burning too long.

What follows is a guided tour through that house – six rooms built from six illusions. Each was raised in the name of clarity, each now flickers in the half-light. The task is not demolition but recognition: to trace the wiring of the Enlightenment's glow before it shorts for good.

FOUR

The Afterimage Effect

Every critique keeps a candle burning for what it claims to extinguish.

The Enlightenment's critics were never its enemies; they were its children blinking in the same light. Nietzsche declared God dead but kept the faith that revelation redeems. Marx dismantled metaphysics but retained its grammar – the promise of emancipation through unveiling. Freud, with equal fervour, unearthed the unconscious only to enthrone it as a new tribunal of truth. Each claimed to shatter illusion, yet each preserved the oldest one: that exposure itself is salvation. To drag a thing into the light was still, for them, to redeem it.

The Enlightenment taught us that illumination is purification, that darkness hides error and light dispels it. Its heretics accepted the premise and merely changed the target. Nietzsche's hammer was a solar instrument; Marx's revolution a sunrise; Freud's couch another confessional. Even the postmodernists – those supposed assassins of reason – never truly escaped its radiance. They replaced truth with play, certainty with deferral, but their theatre remained lit by the same bulb. Irony, too, needs illumination to cast its shadow.

We have confused the act of exposure with the act of understanding. The glare of critique has become our last superstition: the belief that if we can only reveal enough – bias, ideology, trauma, system – the world will right itself. We mistake unveiling for transformation. But the Enlightenment's light was never moral; it was optical. It showed without curing. The modern age has simply multiplied its lamps, bathing every corner of existence in the fluorescence of analysis. We are all critics now, and the world grows dimmer for it.

The afterimage is what remains when the eyes close. It is not the light itself but the echo of its intensity – a memory that persists after the source has gone. Our philosophies are afterimages – attempts to describe a world that once believed illumination could save it. Nietzsche's will, Marx's dialectic, Freud's drive – all are the phosphorescent residues of a belief in light's authority. Even deconstruction, with its elegant refusals, depends on the page's whiteness to make its mark. Every negation bears the outline of what it negates.

Perhaps the task now is not to strike the match again but to study the afterglow – to see how reason lingers even in decay, how faith in progress continues to animate its disproofs. The bulb does not go dark when the switch is flipped; it fades, hums, smoulders. Our institutions, our sciences, our critiques all run on that residual current. We live not in the Enlightenment but in its half-life.

To learn from the afterimage is to accept that there is no outside of the light, no vantage unexposed. The question is not how to destroy it but how to dwell with it – how to see within the lingering haze without mistaking it for dawn. The Enlightenment never ended; it only receded, leaving its glow on everything it touched. The real work begins in that dimness, when the eyes, at last, begin to adjust.

The afterimage fades, but the structure remains. What follows is a tour of that structure – a walk through the rooms where the Enlightenment's light still flickers, where its myths still shape our thought. Step carefully. The floorboards creak. The light is too bright in some places, too dim in others.

PART II

THE

HOUSE OF REASON

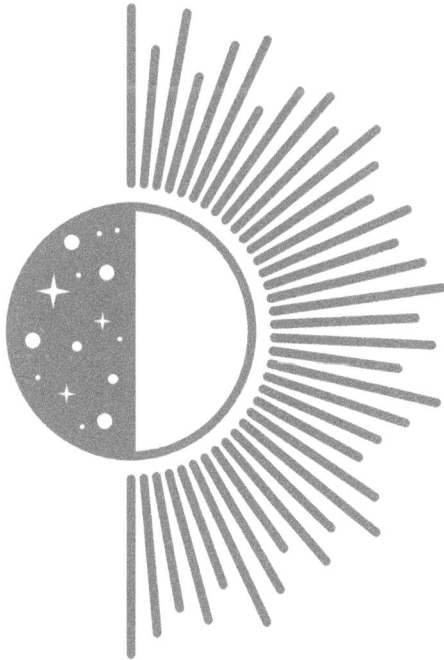

FIVE

Architecture of the Anti-Enlightenment

The Enlightenment built a house for reason. It was elegant, symmetrical, well lit. Each room was designed to contain a foundational myth – objectivity, agency, progress, normality – illusions that still shape how we think and live. The problem was never the craftsmanship but the blueprint: every room assumed a foundation that would not hold. The Anti-Enlightenment project begins by walking through those rooms, tapping the walls, listening for the hollowness that progress painted over.

Each essay in this volume dismantles one of those load-bearing myths – the ideas that promised stability whilst quietly distorting what it means to live and think. Read together, they are less demolition than archaeology, peeling back plaster to reveal the scaffolding beneath.

Step carefully. The floorboards creak. The light is too bright in some places, too dim in others. We'll move slowly, room to room, as the glare begins to fade.

The First Room – Objectivity Is Illusion: The Ritual of Reason

The front door opens onto truth itself. Here, objectivity is exposed not as neutrality but as ritual – an inherited posture masquerading as epistemology. What we call reason often functions as etiquette: a set of agreed-upon manners for managing uncertainty. This essay begins the unlearning by showing that our instruments of clarity are social performances, not mirrors of the real.

The Enlightenment imagined that truth could be purified of perspective, that vision could float free of the body. But every act of observation bears the fingerprints of its observer. What we call objectivity is not a transparent lens but a collective style – a choreography of credibility that makes knowledge look clean. Reason's light is theatrical, not natural; it flatters both performer and audience.

In this room, the walls are bright white, but the paint hides centuries of fingerprints. To touch them is to remember that thinking has always been social, that truth is not a discovery but an agreement we keep re-signing.

Follow the corridor to the next room. The light hums louder there.

The Second Room – Rational Ghosts: The Haunted Machinery of Choice

Beyond the threshold lies politics, built on the myth that the collective can be governed by the arithmetic of individuals. Rational Ghosts traces how democracy's Enlightenment architecture – its equations of choice and will – turned participation into consumption. What remains is not reasoned consensus but a haunted system, possessed by its own abstractions.

The Enlightenment replaced the divine right of kings with the divine right of numbers. Votes became sacraments; consent became ritual. Yet the will of the people is no less spectral than the will of God – it must be invoked to exist. Every election re-summons the ghost, demanding belief in a rational citizen who never quite appears.

In this room, voices echo. Each wall repeats the same chorus in slightly different tones, and somewhere between them the illusion of unity forms. The light is steady but cold – the fluorescence of administration, where reason hums at the frequency of bureaucracy.

Through the far archway, the air grows warmer. The next room measures time itself.

The Third Room – Temporal Ghosts: The Tyranny of the Present

Time forms the corridor connecting every other room. Temporal Ghosts explores how the Enlightenment remade duration into progress, converting the human rhythm of seasons and decay into a single forward arrow. We inhabit that invention still: the anxious present that calls itself the future.

Progress was the Enlightenment's clock: every tick a moral improvement, every tock a step toward perfection. But clocks do not measure time – they produce it. Their regularity teaches the body what 'now' should feel like. Under their discipline, the past becomes waste and the future a warehouse of promise forever deferred.

In this room, the light never changes. The curtains are drawn back, but the view is motionless – a bright horizon painted on the wall. To linger here is to sense that movement itself has become the illusion, that time's straight line is just another corridor built to keep us walking.

Beyond this corridor lies the study – the chamber of the self, and the beginning of the Fourth Room.

The Fourth Room – Against Agency: The Self That Never Was

The corridor narrows and opens into a study. The air is still. Dust floats in the beam of a single lamp, illuminating a desk, a mirror, and a chair left slightly askew – as though its occupant has just stepped away to think. This is the chamber of the self, the Enlightenment's favourite invention and its most enduring myth.

Here sits the autonomous actor: the rational subject imagined to stand apart from circumstance, to decide, to will, to author the world through intention. He was the masterpiece of modern reason – the creature who could sign contracts, cast votes, confess sins, and take responsibility for both virtue and ruin. The Enlightenment required his existence; without him, no promise of liberty or progress could hold.

He was called the individual – a mind luminous enough to guide itself, a body disciplined enough to obey its own commands. From him the new order drew its power: every parliament, every courtroom, every marketplace required his signature. Without this autonomous actor – freely choosing, freely erring – the architecture of reason would have no tenant. Agency was the myth that made the machinery run.

But the longer we remain in this room, the more it feels staged. The books on the shelves are unread, the mirror clouded by breath. The self, it turns out, is not the room's owner but its echo. What we call will is choreography learned from invisible architectures – habits, histories, economies – that move through us and call the movement our own.

In *Against Agency* I argued that this creature never existed. What the Enlightenment celebrated as will was a bookkeeping device: a way to assign praise and blame, debt and duty. Freedom became the solvent that kept moral and economic accounts from coagulating. It was not ontology but audit. The self was invented to balance the ledger.

Under the optical regime of modernity, the individual appeared as a small, portable sun – each person imagined as a self-illuminating point of reason. The metaphor was seductive: if light radiates outward, then responsibility must too. But every lantern needs oil, and the oil was social. The worker's obedience, the voter's consent, the sinner's repentance – all were acts staged to keep the lamp burning. Freedom, rehearsed often enough, began to look like fact.

Agency, in this sense, was never a power but a permission. It existed only within the bandwidth allotted by circumstance. To act required safety, time, and attention – the very resources unevenly distributed by the systems that preached equality of will. The rich man's choice and the poor woman's necessity were labelled with the same word: decision. The Enlightenment turned contingency into culpability and called it justice.

This illusion persists because it flatters both ruler and ruled. To the ruler it offers moral cover: if subjects are autonomous, their suffering is self-authored. To the ruled it offers dignity: if every act is choice, then endurance is heroism. Between those consolations, the fiction endures. We mistake motion for mastery, reflex for reason. The self feels bright because the walls around it are painted white.

Yet the cracks show. Neuroscience, behavioural economics, and ordinary exhaustion converge on the same admission: the self does not steer so much as surf – riding currents of habit, hormone, and history. What we call will is usually momentum remembered too late.

Freedom is *post-factum* narration: a commentary added in subtitles after the scene has already played. We are not authors but annotators of our own conduct.

The alternative is not fatalism. It is responsiveness. Every living thing adjusts to signals, constraints, invitations. Choice emerges in the interval between impulse and inhibition, a flicker of relational awareness. Ethics begins in that flicker. To act responsibly is not to assert control but to remain receptive – to sense the shifting pressure of the world and move with minimal violence through it. Responsiveness is what remains of agency once the theatre lights are turned off. Imagine a conversation where no one rushes to claim the last word, where silence is not absence but attention. Imagine a politics that measures its success not by the clarity of its laws, but by the capacity of its people to listen, adapt, and care.

Seen this way, morality changes key. It ceases to measure sovereignty and begins to measure sensitivity. The question is no longer *Who* caused this? but *Who* is listening? Freedom becomes ecological: the capacity of a system to keep channels of responsiveness open. Politics becomes the tending of those channels – education, rest, trust, time. Every society that throttles them and then blames the exhausted for their silence re-enacts the Enlightenment's oldest joke.

When autonomy fades, a quieter intelligence emerges. The light that once came from the self is replaced by an ambient glow of relation – each consciousness reflecting the others. Responsiveness is that light: diffuse, shared, unowned. To live by it is to give up the dream of being incandescent and learn instead to see by reflection. This is where Dis-Integrationism begins: in the dusk after the empire of agency, when philosophy stops worshipping the lamp and starts attending to what it illuminates only by accident.

Beyond the study, a stair leads upward. The air grows cooler, the light more clinical. Here, the Enlightenment's obsession with measurement and control reaches its apex – the room where the human itself was redesigned for legibility.

The Fifth Room – The Myth of Homo Normalis: The Legible Human

A narrow stair leads upward from the study. The steps are shallow, worn smooth by repetition. At the top: a long gallery lined with mirrors. Their silvering has begun to fade, but the reflections persist – some distorted, others eerily precise. This is the Enlightenment's mirror room, the place where reason learned to see itself and call the image human.

Every empire begins by measuring the bodies it governs. The Enlightenment called its census science: a benevolent catalogue of reason's children. Out of that bright arithmetic emerged *Homo Normalis* – the average man, the mean between extremes, the human smoothed of particularity. He was not a person but a statistical ghost, conjured from the aggregate and imposed back upon the living as ideal. His proportions became our mirrors. His symmetry became our shame.

Before modernity, difference was mostly narrative: saints and sinners, fools and geniuses, each judged within the story that held them. The Enlightenment replaced the parable with the bell curve. Every trait – height, intelligence, virtue – was plotted on a graph, and the midpoint declared holy. Deviation became pathology. Error became identity. The moral imagination of the West learned to worship the centre.

Once deviation could be measured, it could be managed. Hospitals, prisons, schools, and factories aligned themselves to the new geometry of improvement. The ruler and the ruler – the instrument and the monarch – merged. Legibility became the condition for care: to be seen was to be saved, but only if one fit the lens. The rest were distortions, requiring correction or erasure.

The paradox is that normality was never found in nature. It was a bureaucratic invention masquerading as discovery. The average man did not pre-exist the measurement; he emerged from it. The Enlightenment believed it had uncovered a law of human proportion when in fact it had minted a new currency of control. Visibility became virtue. To be known was to be good. The soul was redescribed as data.

This faith in legibility still animates our machines. We call it transparency, we call it inclusion, but the logic is the same: the system that demands to see everything must flatten what it sees. Big Data is only the Enlightenment's census updated to the speed of light. The algorithm inherits the magistrate's stare – omnivident, unblinking, efficient. It judges by correlation, not conviction, but the result is familiar: a world where outliers are dangerous precisely because they confuse the model.

Yet there is an ethical cost to constant illumination. The more visible we become, the less distinct we are. Privacy, opacity, refusal – these are not defects in a social order but its remaining forms of grace. To live otherwise is to confuse detection with understanding, recognition with relation. The dream of full legibility ends, inevitably, in surveillance: the eye that claims to know us better than we can know ourselves.

Against this, Dis-Integrationism proposes not secrecy but subtlety. It does not romanticise obscurity; it restores it as a condition of freedom. Every relation requires a margin of unknowing – a shadow where interpretation can rest. Ethics, under this view, is not the elimination of ambiguity but the care of it. To keep a person partly unread is to keep them possible.

Homo Normalis was the Enlightenment's most flattering illusion: the fantasy that reason could design the human. It offered the comfort of symmetry, the security of averages, the warmth of belonging. But it also made monstrosity inevitable. The moment the middle becomes moral, difference becomes sin. The only way out of that geometry is to step aside from its light – to dwell, as all real bodies do, at the edge of measurement, where the instruments blur and the self stops needing to be squared.

The mirrors flicker as you turn to leave. Each pane reflects another, a recursion of gazes folding in on themselves until form dissolves into shimmer. Here, the Enlightenment's proudest achievement – self-knowledge – becomes its most elegant prison. Beyond these reflections, a stair descends into open air. The roof is gone. The next and final chamber is not a room at all but a threshold where philosophy, stripped of shelter, learns at last to weather.

The Sixth Room – The Discipline of Dis-Integration: Philosophy Without Redemption

The stair descends into air. There is no ceiling now, only the cold, wide sky.

Wind moves through the beams, scattering papers left on a table long ago. The walls, once bright with intention, have crumbled into apertures. This is not quite a ruin, not quite a home – just a space that refuses conclusion. Here the Enlightenment's architecture ends, and something quieter begins.

Every system dreams of repair.

It is the oldest reflex of the Enlightenment mind: the conviction that fracture is failure and that thought exists to mend. Even critique, its most rebellious child, rarely escapes this reflex – expose the flaw, draft the fix, rebuild the edifice stronger than before. The Discipline of Dis-Integration begins when that instinct falters. It does not reject repair out of despair but from precision. The house keeps collapsing because its foundation demands perfection.

To think dis-integratively is to accept that the work of philosophy ends not in renovation but in maintenance. This practice begins where redemption stops – where every promised cure reveals itself as another symptom. The Enlightenment treated reason as a cleansing flame; what remains now are the burn marks, faint but instructive. We can still learn from the residue, but we can no longer pretend to rebuild the fire.

Dis-Integrationism is not ruin-worship; it is composure. It names the art of staying with what breaks instead of blueprinting another illusion. The hyphen matters. It signals deliberation: not collapse into chaos but the chosen spacing between fragments. Where philosophy once sought synthesis, this method cultivates suspension – the ability to hold contradiction without closing it.

In this open chamber, the elements are constant guests. Rain writes on the stone; moss thickens in the corners. To live here is to learn a new rhythm of care. You wipe the table, mend the hinge, patch the roof – not because you believe the structure eternal, but because tending is the only honest relation left to it. This is maintenance as metaphysics: attention without endgame, compassion without teleology.

Two gestures define the craft.

First, naming the seam – tracing where construction meets contingency, where the smooth surface hides its join. Consider, for example, how the ideal of 'objectivity' depends on the unspoken labour of those who clean the lens, who decide what counts as data, who bear the cost of what is left unexamined.

Second, sitting with it – resisting the narcotic of solution, allowing the exposed edge to remain exposed.

Each act defies the Enlightenment's grammar of progress. It replaces the hero's forward stride with the caretaker's return. The gesture is smaller but more exact.

To many, this stance will seem passive. It is not. Maintenance is the invisible labour that allows all motion. Every light that still burns does so because someone cleaned the glass. The dis-integrationist accepts the futility of final repair and, paradoxically, finds in that futility a deeper endurance. There is dignity in upkeep – a quiet ethic of persistence that outlives every revolution's rhetoric.

Beyond redemption, philosophy becomes tactile again. Thought returns to breath, to dust, to the slow pulse of what refuses to be completed. The discipline is simple: tend what you can reach, repair what you touch, leave the rest unpromised. When the architects finally fold their plans, the caretakers will already be at work – patching, sweeping, keeping the place habitable long enough for thought to continue.

This is the final room because it refuses to close. The house of Reason stands behind you, its cracks now visible, its glow now dim. Ahead, there is no blueprint – only the work of tending what remains. There is no door to latch, no ceiling to contain the air. What began in the glare of the Enlightenment ends in the half-light of maintenance – a philosophy that knows its own impermanence and calls that knowledge peace.

SIX

Fault Lines: How Systems Fail by Design

Step back a little. From this height the house of Reason looks intact – columns upright, windows clear, roof-lines sharp against the sky. Yet every wall hums faintly with tension. The cracks are not accidents; they are blueprinted. Instability, in these architectures, is structural.

The Enlightenment imagined complexity as something to be managed, not endured. It wanted the world calculable, outcomes predictable, systems obedient to linear thought. But living systems – political, ecological, psychological – resist straight lines. They bend, loop, self-adjust. When pressed into order, they break in familiar rhythms: collapse, reform, collapse again.

The same physics that governs climate models haunts economies and empires alike. Feedback becomes noise; resilience becomes fragility disguised as strength. Every revolution inherits the logic of the one before it because the blueprint – the dream of mastery – remains untouched.

'Complexity', as the systems theorists note, 'is where ideals go to die'. Yet their death is instructive. Each failure marks the limit of a design that mistook control for care, coherence for truth. The cracks are not curses; they are apertures. Through them, weather enters. Through them, life breathes.

The Anti-Enlightenment learns not to seal these openings but to tend them – to accept that a stable world is a dead one, and that endurance lies not in completion but in the capacity to keep adjusting when perfection fails again.

SEVEN

The Persistence of the Glow

If the house keeps cracking, why do we keep rebuilding it? Habit, perhaps. Or faith in brightness itself.

The Enlightenment taught us to equate light with virtue, clarity with safety. The result is an emotional addiction: we fear the dimness that follows every failure, so we rush to relight the ruins. The rhetoric changes – innovation, reform, disruption – but the gesture is the same. Each new bulb promises a gentler radiance, a smarter grid, a moral wattage that will finally make the world transparent.

Institutions have learned to monetise this glow. *Dataism* sells omniscience as benevolence; moral capitalism packages virtue as a subscription. Universities, corporations, and governments compete not for truth but for luminosity – the appearance of enlightenment. The brighter the branding, the darker the machinery behind it.

The persistence of the glow is psychological as much as structural. It flatters our exhaustion, telling us that illumination will save us from the work of seeing. But brightness without warmth is sterilising; it bleaches nuance, erases texture, blinds as much as it reveals.

What if we stopped mistaking brightness for warmth? What if we accepted that understanding, like comfort, belongs to twilight – to the moments when light softens enough for shadow to re-enter the frame?

The glow will persist, of course. Every era loves its reflection. But we might at least learn to recognise its hum: the gentle, anxious buzz of systems afraid to rest.

Exiting the House of Reason

When you step beyond the threshold, the ground gives slightly underfoot.

Grass has grown through the flagstones; the outline of the house is visible only in memory. The rooms you have walked are still there somewhere – truth, polity, time, self, body, care – but they no longer align. Their symmetry has relaxed into landscape.

Above you, the light has changed. It is no longer the white of revelation but the amber of evening, slanted, patient. The world feels larger not because it is new but because the ceilings are gone.

Behind, the house of Reason continues to crumble with dignity, releasing its dust into the wind. Ahead, there is nothing to rebuild – only to inhabit.

You take a breath. The air smells of rain and iron. This is not enlightenment but weather: a living atmosphere, shifting, partial, real. It will be enough.

Every illumination must fade before perception can begin. The task is not to kindle another flame, but to learn the patience of dusk.

LIVING AFTER THE LIGHT

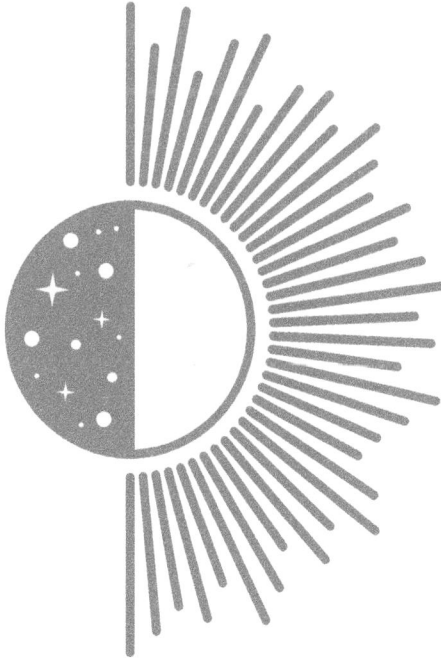

Prelude to Part III – The Light That Remains

Evening does not erase the day; it completes it. The light that lingers after brightness fades is not its opposite but its consequence – the residue of seeing once the will to see has softened. The Enlightenment mistook that residue for error, calling every dimness ignorance, every pause regression. Yet dusk has its own intelligence: it teaches the eyes to widen, the body to slow, the mind to listen.

To live after the light is to inherit its exhaustion. Centuries of radiance have left the air thin, the colours overexposed. We know too much, but mostly of surfaces. Now the world asks for a different sense – one that can perceive contour without conquest, relation without reduction. The task ahead is not to strike another match but to learn how to breathe in the near-dark.

Shadow, once feared as the hiding place of error, becomes the refuge of difference. Here nuance can survive the floodlight; tenderness can persist without proof. The outlines blur, and in that blurring something like compassion returns. The hard distinctions – true and false, sane and mad, pure and impure – begin to soften back into gradients. We start to remember that clarity was never the only virtue, merely the loudest.

Philosophy in the half-light trades certainty for depth. It no longer seeks to illuminate everything at once but to trace what glimmers at the edge of attention. The Anti-Enlightenment does not celebrate darkness for its own sake; it studies how things live within it. The mind, like the pupil, dilates when confronted with obscurity. What was invisible at noon becomes visible at dusk.

This is the discipline of patience – the willingness to wait until meaning reveals itself obliquely, through tone, through texture, through what refuses to be named. It is not withdrawal but calibration. The age of illumination gave us vision as command; the age that follows must rediscover vision as care.

Step carefully. Let your eyes adjust. What remains of light will be enough.

EIGHT

In Praise of Shadow

Darkness is not the negation of light but its remainder – the space that brightness leaves behind when it has finished announcing itself. The Enlightenment taught us to fear that space, to treat shadow as failure, as the retreat of reason. Yet every illumination casts one, and what gathers there is not ignorance but intimacy. Shadow is the condition for depth; without it, the world becomes all surface, a glare too thin to bear weight.

Tanizaki understood this long before we named it post-anything. In his *In Praise of Shadows*, he wrote not as aesthete but as anthropologist of restraint. He saw how a lacquer bowl glows more fully in dim light than in sunlight, how gold leaf needs darkness to breathe, how an empty alcove holds reverence precisely because it conceals. He did not romanticise obscurity; he restored its dignity. Where the West sought visibility as virtue, Tanizaki understood concealment as care – a way of protecting fragility from the violence of exposure.

The Anti-Enlightenment begins in a similar hush. After centuries spent flooding every corner with analysis, we must now learn how to dwell again in partial sight. Obscurity, properly tended, is not the enemy of knowledge but its atmosphere. It permits ambiguity to live long enough to mature into understanding. Clarity too quickly demanded is cruelty; it strips experience before it can ripen.

Consider the cathedral at dusk. The stained glass no longer preaches in colour but hums in silhouette. The nave darkens until sound itself becomes architecture – the shuffle of feet, the slow exhale of wood. Or the city at midnight, when billboards power down and reflections take over for light; windows blink like tired eyes and the street reveals its shape only by the memory of its day. Even the blue glow of a sleeping screen has its lesson: that the technologies of vision cannot rest until we do.

In shadow, hierarchy dissolves. The bright and the dull, the valuable and the broken, all fall into the same soft equality. Here humility is not moral posture but perceptual fact: no single thing dominates, and the eye must wander to find what matters. Obscurity becomes democratic – each object given just enough to be sensed, never enough to be possessed.

The Enlightenment promised that light would set us free; instead it left us overexposed. The task now is not to extinguish illumination but to temper it – to relearn the art of dimming. Shadow teaches pause. It invites the hand to slow before touching, the voice to lower before speaking, the mind to hesitate before concluding. Philosophy, once obsessed with shining, must become an exercise in shading: the modulation of attention rather than its beam.

This is not a plea for ignorance or mysticism. It is a call for proportion. Too much light flattens; too much visibility consumes. The half-lit world offers contour, contrast, the chance to perceive without conquest. To think in shadow is to remember that revelation need not blind, and that sometimes the most honest insight arrives as a whisper, not a glare.

When the glare at last subsides, what remains is gentler but more precise. Thought becomes tactile again; words regain texture. We see not everything, but enough – and for once, enough is all that is required.

NINE

Meditations in the Half-Light

To think in the half-light is not to go gentle into the night. It is to remain awake precisely when the world invites sleep. Darkness is not the end of seeing; it is the test of whether we can still perceive without certainty to steady us. Where the Enlightenment sought dominion through illumination, the half-light demands composure. It is a discipline of staying – of letting perception stretch until it learns to sense by pulse, by echo, by the faint warmth of what endures when vision tires.

In the half-light, philosophy loses its podium. It becomes an act of breathing: slow, repetitive, alive to interruption. One learns to think without conclusion, to feel one's way through ideas like furniture in a dark room – carefully, by memory, aware that the shape of things changes depending on where one stands. A phrase, a doubt, a remembered face: each becomes a kind of landmark. Knowledge is no longer something we own but something that visits, briefly, when the air is still enough to receive it.

The Enlightenment taught us to worship the known, to fill silence with reason until mystery suffocated. But mystery never left; it simply withdrew its trust. To meditate in the half-light is to court that trust again – not to demand answers but to make room for them. The question itself becomes an act of care. Each pause, each hesitation, is a small refusal of violence: a way of saying the world need not yield all at once to understanding.

This is what Meditations on Nothing tried to inhabit – the quiet after the sentence, the lucid moment when meaning dissolves but attention remains. The page becomes a clearing where thought sheds its categories like skin. What lingers is not insight but atmosphere: the hum of being when explanation falls silent. To live there is neither despair nor apathy; it is fidelity to experience unforced.

Sometimes this practice looks ordinary. A hand resting on a windowsill. A breath held before speaking. A decision delayed not out of indecision but out of respect for what has not yet declared itself. The half-light is lived as rhythm more than rule – its ethics closer to music than to law.

The half-light does not console. It clarifies by subtraction. It shows what can survive without ornament, without guarantee. Compassion, endurance, restraint – these are the faculties that adjust best to dimness. They do not seek to banish the dark but to walk beside it. The philosopher here is less a lantern-bearer than a listener, attuned to the subtle acoustics of the unseen.

In this condition, lucidity and humility become the same act. To know something partially is no longer failure but proportion. We discover that understanding deepens only when we stop trying to possess it. Meaning arrives like the dawn: not by conquest, but by degrees.

The half-light is not an ending; it is the hour before beginning. Every shadow, if tended, turns eventually toward morning – not the blinding kind the Enlightenment promised, but a gentler brightness: diffuse, humane, forgiving. The task is to keep that light low enough that we can still see one another within it.

When the eyes adjust, the hands remember what to do.

The half-light teaches not what to see, but how to stay – with imperfection, with fracture, with what continues despite itself. Thought slows until it becomes touch, and the abstract returns to the tactile. What began as philosophy turns quietly into maintenance: the daily art of keeping what remains from falling further apart.

In this dimness, care becomes the only coherent grammar left to us. Not as cure, not as redemption, but as rhythm – a steady, deliberate attendance to what still flickers. After illumination fades, this is what thinking looks like: a cloth folded, a hinge mended, a sentence rewritten by hand until it holds.

TEN

Maintenance Ethics: Care without Redemption

After the glare fades, what remains is work. Not the heroic kind – the kind that photographs well – but the slow, repetitive tending that keeps the ordinary intact. A light bulb replaced. A table wiped. A sentence re-written until it stops trembling. Maintenance is philosophy after the crisis: the discipline of staying with what cannot be perfected.

For centuries, ethics was built on the grammar of salvation. Every moral system promised ascent: from sin to grace, from ignorance to enlightenment, from error to improvement. Even the secular inherited this reflex. We still imagine virtue as progress and failure as relapse. But the world does not move upward. It drifts, settles, decays, renews. Maintenance accepts that motion as condition rather than problem.

To maintain is to admit dependence. Nothing lasts by itself. Entropy is not enemy but partner – the reminder that attention must be paid again and again. Each act of care is provisional, destined to unravel, and therefore honest. The value lies not in preservation but in recurrence. A mended hinge will loosen; the hinge is not the point. The point is the hand returning.

In this sense, maintenance is not the opposite of philosophy but its continuation by other means. The question shifts from What is right? to What still holds? Thought bends toward the practical without surrendering its dignity. A clear surface, a stable structure, a repaired sentence – each becomes an instance of coherence wrested from disorder, temporary yet meaningful.

Dis-Integrationism calls this the ethic of non-redemption. It refuses the Enlightenment's obsession with rescue – the belief that the right idea, the right law, the right innovation will finally save us. To maintain is to let go of that fantasy without collapsing into despair. It is to act without promise, to repair without prophecy. The moral gesture lies in the doing, not the deliverance.

This ethic does not require serenity. It often feels like fatigue performed faithfully. The custodian sweeping after everyone has left; the nurse adjusting a patient's blanket at 3 a.m.; the friend answering one more call. These are not metaphors for care – they are its definition. Maintenance is what ethics looks like when stripped of spectacle. It does not redeem the world; it keeps it habitable.

Because maintenance is shared, it breeds reciprocity. Every act of tending presumes another's future use. To patch, to clean, to preserve is to imagine an unseen other who will touch what you have touched. Care circulates; it cannot be owned. In this circulation lies the faint political hope of Dis-Integrationism: not revolution, not restoration, but continuity.

The task, then, is modest. Tend what you can reach. Repair what you touch. Leave the rest unpromised. Perfection was always a form of violence; maintenance is its undoing. It restores scale to meaning, returning philosophy to the pace of breath. When we accept that the bulb will burn out again, that the hinge will loosen, that thought itself will fade, we begin to understand care as endurance rather than cure.

And in that endurance – quiet, repetitive, unspectacular – the world remains possible.

ELEVEN

After the Enlightenment

Every dawn believes itself the first. The Enlightenment was no exception. It declared itself the age of beginnings, the hour when darkness fled and truth at last stood visible. But light is never innocent. What it reveals, it also invents. We built our world inside that brilliance until we could no longer tell whether we were seeing clearly or simply burning slowly.

Now the bulb has dimmed. The circuits of progress hum with fatigue. Our instruments glow long after conviction has gone out, illuminating the ruins out of habit. This is not collapse; it is afterglow – the lingering of systems that can still produce light but no longer warmth. To live after the Enlightenment is to dwell in that phosphorescence: the faint persistence of an idea that once mistook itself for nature.

Here the work of philosophy changes tense. It stops predicting and begins attending. The future ceases to be a destination and becomes an atmosphere – something to breathe carefully rather than to conquer. The question is no longer what comes next, but how to remain in relation when next has no meaning.

Dis-Integrationism names that relation. It is the practice of composure within exhaustion, of clarity without conquest. It asks us to trade the fantasy of renewal for the discipline of return. We sweep the same floors, tend the same fractures, revisit the same paradoxes. It is not futility; it is fidelity – the slow devotion to what remains when salvation retires.

The Anti-Enlightenment is often misheard as rejection. It is not rebellion against reason but its reckoning. Every age believes its clarity unique; every aftermath learns that clarity was always provisional. To think after the Enlightenment is not to curse the light but to notice the burn marks, to study their pattern, to learn how not to repeat them.

If the Enlightenment was a flash, this moment is its reflection on water: rippled, refracted, alive. In that wavering image lies a quieter radiance – less revelation than recognition. The world still glows, but differently now, lit by the modest fire of those who maintain it.

The task is no longer to begin again, but to keep the beginning open. To walk through the ruins without turning them into relics. To practice lucidity as care, not conquest. The light we inherit is weaker, yes, but finally humane. It no longer promises redemption; it allows us to see each other.

Epilogue – The Continuing Light

No philosophy ends cleanly. Even this one, written against finality, trails its own filaments – threads of thought still humming after the words go still. What begins in refusal must end in continuation: the slow, unfinished labour of seeing again.

If the Enlightenment's promise was illumination without limit, the Anti-Enlightenment offers something smaller and truer – a practice of shared lucidity. Not brilliance, but bearing. Not knowledge as possession, but understanding as relation. The light remains, but diffused across many hands, each tending its own small flame.

These pages are not a closure but a handoff. The half-light belongs to whoever chooses to work within it – to the reader who keeps thinking after the book ends, who mends, questions, sustains. In that persistence, philosophy survives exactly as it should: not as monument, but as maintenance.

So take what still glows. Carry it carefully. It was never meant to blind, only to help you find your way.

Philosophy ends, as it should, where the hand steadies the flame.

APPENDICES

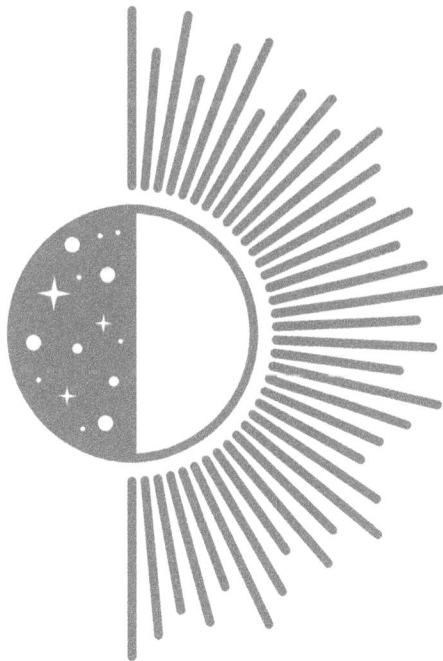

Appendix A: Timeline of the Anti-Enlightenment Project

Essay / Publication	Central Claim	Key Myth Disassembled
Against Agency: *The Fiction of the Autonomous Self*	The self's freedom is an accounting fiction; will is choreography, not command.	The Sovereign Individual
The Discipline of Dis-Integration: *Philosophy Without Redemption*	Philosophy becomes maintenance; redemption is replaced by care.	The Redemptive Order
The Illusion of Light: *Thinking After the Enlightenment*	The unifying reflection and afterimage: illumination as economy, care as inheritance.	The Myth of Illumination
The Myth of Homo Normalis: *Archaeology of the Legible Human*	Normality is the bureaucratic invention of control.	The Measurable Human
Objectivity Is Illusion: *An Operating Model of Social and Moral Reasoning*	Objectivity is not detachment but ritualised etiquette.	The Truth of Reason
Rational Ghosts: *Why Enlightenment Democracy Was Built to Fail*	Reason's politics collapses into arithmetic; democracy becomes haunted by its own abstraction.	The Collective Will
Temporal Ghosts: *The Tyranny of the Present*	Progress imprisons time within the ideology of improvement.	The Arrow of Time

Appendix B: Further Reading in the Half-Light

These are not citations, but invitations—texts that breathe within the same atmosphere.

GENEALOGIES & COUNTER-ENLIGHTENMENTS
- Theodor Adorno & Max Horkheimer, *Dialectic of Enlightenment*
- Michel Foucault, *Discipline and Punish*
- Bruno Latour, *We Have Never Been Modern*
- Friedrich Nietzsche, *The Gay Science*
- Thomas Kuhn, *The Structure of Scientific Revolutions*

ETHICS OF MAINTENANCE & CARE
- María Puig de la Bellacasa, *Matters of Care*
- Joan Tronto, *Moral Boundaries*
- Shannon Mattern, *Maintenance and Care*
- Steven Jackson, "Rethinking Repair"

ILLUMINATION, SHADOW, AND AESTHETICS
- Jun'ichirō Tanizaki, *In Praise of Shadows*
- Susan Sontag, *Regarding the Pain of Others*
- Byung-Chul Han, *The Burnout Society*
- John Berger, *Ways of Seeing*

MODERN DESCENDANTS OF THE LIGHT
- Donna Haraway, *Staying with the Trouble*
- Timothy Morton, *Dark Ecology*
- Bernard Stiegler, *Technics and Time*

Colophon

This book was composed in Arno Pro.

Page design and layout were executed in Adobe InDesign.

Cover design executed in Adobe Illustrator.

Printed and bound independently in the country of distribution.

Published by *Philosophics Press*, an imprint of Microglyphics.

This project was written without institutional patronage or academic appointment. It was composed in the intervals between paid work, sustained by curiosity and fatigue in equal measure.

Philosophy, like maintenance, survives through attention rather than infrastructure.

Philosophics Press exists to keep that attention intact–to publish works that would otherwise be lost between the university's walls and the market's noise.

Design and typography follow the same ethic: restraint over spectacle, legibility over ornament. The pages are meant to breathe. The half-light belongs as much to the reader as to the writer.

About the Author

Bry Willis is an independent philosopher whose work examines the exhausted metaphysics of modernity. Writing outside institutional structures, Willis approaches philosophy as a practice of maintenance rather than mastery – attending to what persists when systems fail. The Anti-Enlightenment Essays trace the afterlives of reason: how Enlightenment ideals of progress, agency, objectivity, and normality became technologies of control. Each essay dismantles a foundational myth of modern life, not to replace it with another certainty but to create space for thought that refuses redemption. Willis's method, Dis-Integrationism, rejects the demand for synthesis. Instead of assembling fragments into coherent wholes, it tends the fractures – treating philosophy as the discipline of staying with what breaks. This approach draws from systems theory, critical philosophy, and the ethics of care, whilst maintaining a commitment to lucid prose accessible beyond academic circles. In addition to philosophy, Willis works at the intersection of design, typography, and the material culture of ideas. The Illusion of Light reflects this – a book designed to be held, marked, and returned to, embodying the argument that thought survives through attention rather than authority. *He offers sincere apologies in the event of any misrepresented works.*

The Illusion of Light serves as the prelude to these works – the threshold through which the Anti-Enlightenment project first coheres.

Note on the Text

The essays summarised in Part II are published open-access through Zenodo and PhilArchive. This introduction was written not as commentary but as synthesis – a sustained meditation on the limits of reason and the persistence of care. The six essays remain independent works; together they form the Anti-Enlightenment corpus.

Other Titles by Bry Willis

Books:

    Meditations on Nothing: Notes Before Existence   ISBN: 978-0-9710869-5-1
    Meditations on Nothing: A Companion Guide   ISBN: 978-0-9710869-6-8

The Anti-Enlightenment Essays:

    Rational Ghosts: Why Enlightenment Democracy Was Built to Fail (2025)
    Objectivity Is Illusion: An Operating Model of Social and Moral Reasoning (2025)
    Temporal Ghosts: The Tyranny of the Present (2025)
    Against Agency: The Fiction of the Autonomous Self (2025)
    The Myth of Homo Normalis: Archaeology of the Legible Human (2025)
    The Discipline of Dis-Integration: Philosophy Without Redemption (2025)

Essays are available as open-access publications through Zenodo and PhilArchive.

Connect

Further work: philosophics.blog
Inquiries: talk@philosophics.blog *or* microglyphics@gmail.com

PHILOSOPHICS PRESS

Philosophics Press publishes works that inhabit the fault lines between philosophy, literature, and design. Founded as an imprint of Microglyphics, it exists to sustain thought outside the economies of visibility and prestige – to print, quite literally, what persists when systems fail.

www.ingramcontent.com/pod-product-compliance
Lightning Source LLC
Chambersburg PA
CBHW081403270326
41930CB00015B/3399